For my friend Mandy
with love,

'Do not be anxious about
anything, but in everything by
prayer and petition with
thanksgiving, present your
requests to God.'

Philippians 4:6-7

Nancy Hoffmann

2008

"Give your worries to the LORD.
He will take care of you."
Psalm 55:22

Other Bestmann/Bunnell books:
"Where Does God Sleep, Momma?"
"Plant Your Dreams, My Child"
"Nana, Will You Write Me From Heaven?"
"The Only True Incredible me!"

**Visit us at
www.bestmannbooks.com**

Printed in the United States of America

International Standard Book Number 1-890398-00-4

A Child Said
A Prayer
Tonight

written by
Nancy Bestmann

illustrated by
Gini Bunnell   calligraphed by
Martha Rippere

A child said a prayer tonight and all the heavens were still.

Our Heavenly Father listened close
to hear the child's will....

"Come Lord Jesus,
I want my grandpa
to get well soon ...."

so he can give me hugs and kisses.

Thank you. Please. Amen.

Love, Katilin

A simple prayer
from Katilin's heart
a prayer of hope and faith
For even little children know
God listens when they pray.

He listens when
His children speak,
He knows their wants,
their needs,
their fear

He longs to see
their growing faith
and cares about
each heartfelt tear.

Katilin prayed a prayer that night.
It was heard in heaven above.

The Lord delights in all His children

For He's a God of love.